HITTING HOT

HITTING HOT

IVAN LENDL'S 14-DAY TENNIS CLINIC

IVAN LENDL
and

GEORGE MENDOZA
with photographs by Walter Iooss, Jr.

RANDOM HOUSE NEW YORK

Library of Congress Cataloging-in-Publication Data
Lendl, Ivan, 1960–
  Hitting hot: Ivan Lendl's 14-day Tennis Clinic

  1. Tennis. I. Mendoza, George. II. Title.
GV995.L437 1986   796.342   86-3277
ISBN 0-394-55407-8

2 3 4 5 6 7 8 9

First Edition

Book Design by Lilly Langotsky

To my mother and father
I. L.

For my son, Ryan
G. M.

AUTHOR'S NOTE

Although Ivan Lendl lives only minutes away from my home along the Connecticut shore, his manager, Jerry Solomon, asked me very casually to meet the world's number-one tennis star for the first time in Antwerp, Belgium, where he was engaged in a major tournament. No stranger to the peripatetic life, I quickly packed my bags and found myself journeying more than three thousand miles to meet the young man I admired more than any other tennis player in the world.

I was not disappointed. Ivan Lendl is a unique human being; he is shy, warm, keenly realistic, boyish, patient, and extremely polite, and his humor is disarming. Jerry had warned me that whenever Ivan gets bored he utters the words, "I'm hungry." Hours passed, our interviews stretched through days and nights, and meanwhile Ivan won the European Champions' Championship. Not at any time did Ivan say the words "I'm hungry." Of course, I confess, we did a lot of talking over Ivan's enormous bowls of pasta.

Ivan Lendl is a great champion and a determined spirit. My son, Ryan, who appears with Ivan in this book, knows how deeply we have been touched by this man. I know you will be too.

George Mendoza

This book would not have been possible without the efforts of Jerry Solomon, Ivan's manager; Mike Cohn, our literary agent; Howard Kaminsky, Publisher of Random House; and our editor, Derek Johns. We would also like to thank Larry Mullins, Project Manager of Gleneagles Country Club; Chuck Narvin, Tennis Pro at Gleneagles; and Marisa D'Amico, Tennis Coordinator of ProServ.

I. L. and G. M.

Photographs by: Walter Iooss, Jr.
Editorial consultant: Rick Tetzeli
Consultant: Alexis Castorri
Ivan's student: Ryan Mendoza
Tennis outfits by Adidas
Photographed at Gleneagles Country Club,
   Delray Beach, Florida

CONTENTS

INTRODUCTION

Tennis has always been in my blood, but that doesn't mean it's always been easy going. When I was very young, my parents couldn't figure out what to do with me. My father was ranked in the top fifteen among Czechoslovakian men, and my mother was ranked second among Czechoslovakian women. They spent a lot of time practicing at the local club, and since they couldn't very well leave me at home, they took me along. Then they had to figure out where to put me while they practiced. At first they thought they could just leave me in a courtside seat. Well, being two years old and curious, I naturally hated that idea, and as soon as I saw that they were involved in their practice I'd climb down and wander around the club. It was a small place, but somehow I managed to get myself lost every time. Their next tactic to keep me happy while they played was to bring my little wagon and a couple of toys, in the hope that I would play in the wagon while they played tennis. Well, that didn't work either. I was energetic and noisy, and once I even tipped over the wagon.

Finally, my mother tied me to the net post so that I wouldn't run anywhere. This gave me a chance to watch my parents play. But instead I played with a wooden paddle given to me by Mr. Zeman, the man who later gave me my first real tennis racket. I'd just swing that wooden paddle at any tennis balls that came my way, and I would have run after them if I hadn't been tied to the post.

As I got a bit older, I spent more and more time around the tennis club, until, when I was six, I was under the coach's nose so much that he had to let me in on some of the classes. I had to watch for most of the lesson and pick up balls while the older kids got the regular instruction. But my turn came at the end, and I would hit for as long as the coach would stay out there with me. I still remember those impromptu lessons, as well as the hours of waiting that preceded them.

Each coach supervised a team of players. Once I was old enough to be fully accepted into a team, I had a regular playing schedule. In the winter, there wasn't all that much time, maybe an hour and a half four times a week. But at least I had good and regular coaching and a specific time to be at the club. And I didn't let the limited winter schedule keep me down. Any time there was an open court, I went on it. Any time there was an opponent free, I'd play him. I was beating everyone in my age group, so I mostly looked to play kids in the age group above me. And when summertime came, I was on the court all day. When I was starting out, the most important thing was to get on that court as often as possible, and as a result I found myself playing kids of all ages. It didn't matter, as long as they could play tennis.

You see, even though I didn't know then that I would be a champion, I wanted to play all the time. Not because I thought tennis might bring me fame and fortune, but because it was absolutely my favorite thing to do. I hope that's why you play tennis, and why you're reading this book. Of course I had dreams of being a champion, and there's nothing wrong with that sort of dream. But what kept me going through all the hard times, and what's allowed me to work so hard on improving my game, is the love I've always had for this sport. Everyone has dreams of glory, but if you want to realize those dreams you've got to be able to put them aside while you work hard at something you love.

And that's what this book is all about; working hard at what you love. The fourteen-day clinic that follows is designed for the player who is willing to make sacrifices to improve his game. We will cover every aspect of the game, from ground strokes to volleys, from strategy to proper dietary habits. I will tell you what has worked for me, and in some cases what has worked for others. But most of all I'm interested in presenting the game I call hitting hot, a relentless all-court pressure game that is coming to dominate modern-day tennis.

I have worked hard to get where I am. But I've enjoyed the journey, and this book is my chance to help you along. Good luck. I hope you'll have as much fun as I have. And who knows, maybe you too will find that you have tennis in your blood.

HITTING HOT

DAY ONE:

GROUND STROKES—
FOREHAND AND BACKHAND

Ground strokes are the foundation of anyone's game. They establish the tempo of a match. They are your main tools for setting up an opponent, allowing you to get to net for the knockout, once you've established baseline superiority.

When I was young and hanging around my parents' club in Czechoslovakia, I spent many an afternoon at the backboard, just banging ground strokes against that wall, time after time after time. Not the most exciting memory, perhaps, but those days formed the foundation of my ground strokes today. The point is that you can never practice your ground strokes enough. There are always new ways to make your forehand or backhand a more effective weapon. I enjoy hitting both strokes now. But my backhand has only recently caught up to my forehand, and there was a time, even after I reached the professional level, when I had to cover for my backhand.

Only through hours and hours of hard work, of listening to suggestions and trying new variations was I able to improve my backhand to the point where I can enjoy it as much as my forehand. And when I say practice, I mean time spent carefully analyzing your strokes, deciding what might be wrong and why, and then allowing yourself to practice through some horrible mistakes. Remember, through observing your mistakes you'll improve, even though sometimes you may get really embarrassed and wonder, as I have, How in the world could I have hit something as bad as that last shot?

FOREHAND

On to the strokes, then. On the forehand I use what might be described as a semiwestern grip. The V between my index finger and thumb comes at the back bevel on the top of the racket handle. The index finger is extended up and across the grip. The fingers should not be in too tight. A hammer grip will lock your elbow, causing strain while costing you flexibility. (Any grip formed at rest, of course, is a bit deceptive, since your fingers tighten as you lean into the swing.)

Find a place on the handle where you feel comfortable. You need not slip your hand all the way down the handle, or choke all the way up. I choke up just a bit, because I have good racket control there. But you should experiment, finding a place that gives you racket control with proper fluidity.

While I probably hit one of the hardest forehands in tennis right now, I don't hit it with overwhelming topspin

The grip you use is very important. On the forehand I use the semiwestern grip, which gives me more topspin, more control, and more penetration and depth.

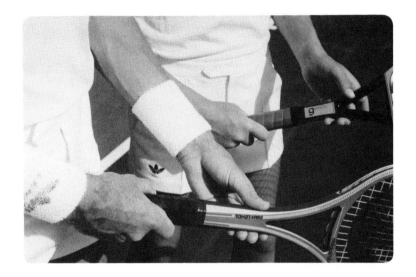

or excessively flat. I want a weapon that can be consistent and overwhelming at the same time. Many of my points are won by setting up an opponent with a series of carefully placed, fairly conservative forehands until he finally gives me a short ball to put away.

There is no single right or wrong way to stroke the forehand. I use a controlled loop for my backswing. Others choose to go straight back without the loop. I believe the loop gives you a greater sense of timing, but I also know that it can be perfected only after a great deal of practice.

At any rate, as you move into the forward part of your stroke you will swing up to and through the ball. This will provide natural topspin, which is heightened by the western or semiwestern grip. Brush up the back of the ball, rather than snapping over it. By hitting through it as you brush up, you hold the ball on the racket strings and get greater control. I come up the back of the ball very

strongly and often wind up with the racket face way above my head. But it's more important to drive through the ball than to snap up harshly, especially as you develop your topspin forehand.

You should be able to hit both a slice and a topspin backhand. Although some great players (Bjorn Borg, for

BACKHAND

Of all the strokes, the most natural is the forehand drive. Note the follow-through: racket head up, butt down.

his topspin, and Ken Rosewall, for his slice, come to mind) have succeeded by using one or the other, in general you need both.

My backhand grip finds the knuckle of my index finger atop the leading edge of the racket handle. My index finger is not spread the way it is on the forehand, and the fingers are tight together but comfortable. I use my backhand grip (commonly called the continental) for all my strokes except the baseline forehand.

The power of the backhand comes from the uncoiling of the shoulders. Start low and end up high. Hit the ball before it gets beyond your shoulder; otherwise you'll be late with the shot.

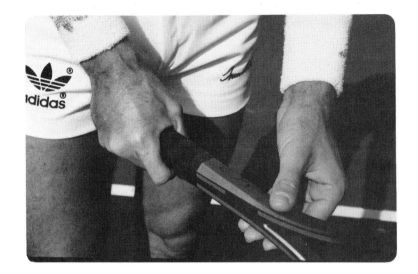

I use my backhand grip (commonly called the continental) for all my strokes except the baseline forehand.

Again, the key to the swing is to start out low and end up high. Sometimes I am so low on my backhand that my knee actually scrapes the ground. In many ways, the backhand is the more natural of the two strokes. After all, what is the only punch outlawed in boxing? The backhand, because the power that comes from uncoiling the shoulders is considered too dangerous. Nevertheless, the backhand is often the weaker stroke at the amateur level. There may be several reasons for weak backhands, but the most common mistake occurs when people wait too long on the ball. The backhand must be met way out in front of the body, even farther so than the forehand. If the ball has a chance to come in on your body, you'll find yourself in a defensive position, unable to uncoil your shoulder turn. The ball is playing you, rather than you playing it, and in that position it's impossible to generate any topspin.

And topspin is essential in today's game. While Borg must be credited with making topspin necessary, his excessive top may not be right for everyone. I think you need different amounts of topspin in different situations. For instance, when you close in on a short ball, you want a slighter topspin that will keep the ball low while sending it deep. But in a baseline rally, you can rely on a heavier topspin to maintain a consistent backcourt game obviously aimed at wearing down your opponent until he makes a mistake.

But don't sacrifice hitting through the ball. High-speed photographs show that a ball literally squashes up onto the racket strings during a stroke. No matter how tightly your racket is strung, it serves as a trampoline for the ball. For a split second, you have complete control of the ball on your racket. So take advantage of that time and stroke through the ball.

That's Day One. Make sure that you're comfortable with your grips, and then practice your forehand and backhand swings until you are hitting the ball well consistently.

DAY TWO:
MORE GROUND STROKES

When I first started playing tennis seriously, my greatest problem was footwork. I've always been tall and thin, and there were times when I wasn't well coordinated. When I was twelve, and again at fifteen, I had real problems. I would run around the court like a stumblebum scarecrow. Even though I outgrew these problems, I was still poor at footwork by the time I reached the pros. Again, hard work and lots of repetitive practice helped my running game.

You can talk all you want about stationary, idealized ground strokes, but in a match you rarely get the opportunity to use them. You have to be able to get to the ball first with quick movement and anticipation. This sets up a stationary stroke. You really only hit on the run in an emergency. Today we'll look at how to do that, as well as how to hit the high backhand.

RUNNING FOREHAND

The running forehand is one of my favorite shots. The forehand drive can be your most potent weapon. Just as your opponent thinks he has you on the defensive, running across the court to reach a wide ball, you can respond with a solid drive to pass him for a winner. The running forehand drive offers you lots of possibilities; it's just a matter of getting down a few basics and making the right choice as to placement.

The first and most important part of the forehand drive is footwork. Run to the ball with a shortened backswing and with your shoulders already turned. Set up on the back foot, and meet the ball out in front. Get into position with big steps, but as you close in on the ball, shorten your step so as to steady yourself.

The running forehand drive can be very useful in desperate situations. I use it when I'm driven wide by an opponent's approach shot. As he comes to net, I drive the ball down the line, extending my follow-through in the direction I want the ball to go.

The running forehand drive may be used in a variety of ways. In addition to hitting deep and down the line, you can bring the ball crosscourt, both deep and short. The short crosscourt is possible with a short backswing and a quick upward snap across your body, which creates wicked topspin. When you hit deep and crosscourt, you should extend your follow-through while trying to cut down on the snap across your body. Your topspin will come more from an extended follow-through than from the snap that brought the short ball down. If you're hitting deep, you need to rely on more than just your arm.

The running backhand drive is governed by the same principles. Shorten your backswing, run in strides and then quick steps, and be sure to set up so that you can meet the ball out in front. The deep shots should be hit with the same emphasis on stroking through the ball, while the short shots require a great roll of the wrist for maximum topspin. Be sure to get the shoulders around on the backhand. Although you may be able to get away with an open stance on the wrong foot on the forehand, the backhand swing is too weak to be consistent without the help of a good shoulder turn and proper setup.

RUNNING BACKHAND

TAKING THE BALL ON THE RISE

On the running forehand, follow through in the direction of the ball.

I'd like to emphasize here the importance of taking the ball on the rise. First of all, taking the ball on the rise allows you to make use of your opponent's pace, making it unnecessary for you to try to generate all the pace on your own. Second, taking the ball on the rise allows you to dictate play. You give your opponent less time to get to net and less time to recover for each shot. Third, taking the ball on the rise cuts down the effect of your opponent's spin. If you can take a topspinner's ground strokes and meet them on the rise, before they have a chance to nail you deep behind the baseline, you'll take away one of his main strengths.

When hitting the backhand slice, imagine that you are carving a bowl. In the last photo in this sequence my racket arm is beginning to come up again.

How do you hit the ball on the rise? First of all, get those knees bent. If you're stiff-kneed, you'll be leaning awkwardly forward, reaching for the ball and using your arms instead of getting your whole body into the shot. Second, meet the ball out in front. Third, get your whole body into the shot, driving through the ball. A good drill for learning to hit the ball on the rise is to take several steps

inside the baseline and hit your ground strokes from this position. This forces you to meet the ball on the rise, while at the same time emphasizing the use of topspin to keep the ball in play.

BACKHAND SLICE

When I'm not in position to hit a backhand drive, I will hit a backhand slice. It is a strong defensive shot that can save you if you are too late to generate good topspin. Start high, come down across the back of the ball, and finish up high again. It's as if you are carving a bowl; don't just hit down on the ball, as so many players do without success. Finish the bowl by coming up again at the end.

One of the most difficult shots to hit in tennis is the high backhand. Try to avoid it at all costs—good footwork usually does the trick. The shot is very awkward and requires a steady hand. First of all, shorten the back-swing, not letting the racket wrap around your head. Then keep your wrist firm. As it's unlikely that you'll be able to get any topspin on a ball that high, stroke straight through the ball rather than trying to brush up the back. And meet the ball out in front, with your shoulders fully turned. Don't make the mistake of hitting down on the ball, for this will drive it into the net. Instead, punch the ball like a volley, driving your follow-through.

Let me add a few words here about conditioning. I build up my stamina by running, stretching, and doing sprints for one or two hours a day over the Christmas break, but the rest of the year I concentrate on developing speed. By running lines, doing wind sprints, and taking on friends in forty-yard dashes, you can work on your speed just as you work on a stroke. Speed around the court makes all the difference in a match. You need to work on your conditioning. As you'll see when we get more involved in conditioning later, there's no magic trick to getting in shape.

That's Day Two. Get your partner to feed you wide forehands and backhands and practice returning them both down the line and crosscourt. And run!

DAY THREE:

SERVE

For some reason, my serve has always come easily. When I come back from Christmas break it takes a while for all my other strokes to get in the groove, but my serve comes back right away. In fact, it is sometimes better after a long break, for a year of pro tennis can take its toll on the strength of my arm.

Starting out, of course, I had to learn all the strokes. The ones that came easiest were the serve and the volley. Then came the forehand, and finally, finally, my backhand came straggling along. At any rate, I developed my serve early on, and while it has always defied convention, it is natural for me. The only word of warning I would give you about my serve is that I toss the ball very high. You might want to keep your toss a little lower, since it's difficult to time a dropping ball.

Your own tennis game is probably a combination of strokes you learned easily and strokes you picked up

only after a lot of practice and trial and error. Look at those strokes that came easily. Are you comfortable with them? Are you doing them the way you always have because they're good or because you've never tried anything else? You've got to know why you hit your strokes the way you do. Falling into comfortable habits isn't necessarily bad: look at my serve. But falling into comfortable bad habits is harmful. So take a step away and see if those old habits can't use a bit of remodeling.

I use my backhand grip on my serve. Many players do, for the backhand grip creates the spin you need. We'll

The serve should be a fluid action. For your follow-through, your racket arm should come across your body. This action will bring your back foot forward and into the court, ready for your next shot.

go into different ways to use spin later on. For now, I want to concentrate on a few crucial elements of the serve.

Many players forget about their toss. Practice it while going through the whole motion of the serve. Practicing the toss without the rest of the motion is useless, since your shoulders pull your toss around.

The toss arm shouldn't be hurried. Some people almost lock their elbows and come straight up, stiffly, while others prefer a looser, arced toss. Whatever you do, be sure that your toss is relaxed and that you toss the ball to the same place every time. No matter how fluid your swing, a toss that's all over the place will throw it off balance.

The service motion has three phases, like the acceleration of a car. The toss and initial pendulum motion backward are the first gear. The racket swings up and drops into backscratch position in second gear, while the knees dip forward into the court. Finally, you explode into third gear, as the knees and racket come up and you go after the ball.

Brush up the back of the ball for spin. When you snap up, go after the ball with everything you've got. You should certainly be on the tips of your toes, and many servers get higher than that. Look at Boris Becker and the enormous force he gets into his serve by snapping up so hard that he is entirely off the ground at contact. Ideally, you will meet the ball at the peak of the toss or, as I do, just as it's beginning to fall. But no matter where it is, you should be fully extended, throwing your entire body up and after the ball. The combination of this forward and upward thrust, along with the spin you get from brushing up the back of the ball, creates a successful spin serve.

A server in motion seems graceful, and yet when you look at still photographs of servers, they always seem so awkward, elbows high in the air, racket pointing at the ground as it comes across the body. You might think that awkward pose implies a bad serve; but in fact it is the result of a strong and necessary wrist snap. The wrist snap counters your upward spin motion with a downward power motion.

I am entirely in agreement with the American custom of hitting hundreds and hundreds of practice serves. But try practicing several different types of serve. Meet the ball at different spots, tossing behind your head for greater spin snap or "kick" serve, and tossing farther out in front for a flatter serve. Work on a second serve that uses plenty of spin. Serve at targets placed in the service box corners. Try serving from three feet behind the baseline; the added distance will force you to snap up for spin. So while your service practice should reinforce your customary serve, it should also involve experimentation with other serves that might be useful at certain times.

DAY FOUR:

OVERHEAD AND LOB

The lob and overhead are always paired for teaching purposes. The overhead seems the more aggressive of the pair. Certainly there is little more satisfying than winning a point or a match on an overwhelming, soundly hit overhead smash. And the overhead *seems* so simple: all you have to do is squash a ball that's a couple of feet from the net. But in fact this stroke causes players at all levels great anguish. Why is it that the overhead seems so hard at the crucial moments of the match? Why is it that the ball chooses those times to hit the racket frame instead of the strings?

I think part of the difficulty with the overhead lies in the fact that we all assume we'll put away each and every one. And so does everyone watching. Missing an overhead is the most glaring error a player can make. And afterward, there's nowhere to hide.

The lob, on the other hand, seems primarily a defensive weapon. But that's not always the case. The offensive lob is one of the most devastating weapons in the game.

In the finals of the 1985 U.S. Open, I entered the third set fairly confident that I was on my way to my first Open championship. But John McEnroe was playing as tough as always. He was serving at 4–4, and I'd managed to get to 15–40. But he won the next point on a service winner to get within one point of sending the game to deuce. At 30–40 I could either get myself into a position to serve out the match and tournament, or I could let him back into the game. He came to net on a deep serve to my backhand and then volleyed my return deep but within reach. I moved toward the ball, disguising my backswing carefully, and put up a deep and unreachable topspin lob. There was nothing he could do. The game was mine, the tournament just a game away. And as I walked back to my chair, there was something satisfying about having clinched the championship with that deceptive shot. I was winning the Open with style, with the grace epitomized by the lob and the power represented by the overhead.

OVERHEAD

Your overhead preparation should be as consistent and early as possible. Most mistakes on the overhead are the result of poor timing, which is avoidable if you have good racket preparation. As soon as the lob is up, get into position and bring the racket back behind your head. I don't drop the head of the racket down my back right away, preferring instead to wait and "dip and throw" at

the ball. This enables me to wind up into my smash, generating a shoulder turn similar to that in the serve. As with the serve, the overhead should be met at full extension.

I don't worry too much about placing the overhead, other than trying to "hit it where they ain't," as the old baseball expression goes. If your preparation and footwork are good and you meet the ball at full extension, that should be the end of the point.

One final point about the overhead. As with the serve, push off from your back foot and bring it forward

Most mistakes on the overhead are the result of poor timing, which is avoidable if you have good racket preparation.

through the shot, provided the ball is in front of you. However, taking an excellent deep lob you may find it necessary to "jackknife" your legs in order to get higher and thus generate the power to successfully bring the ball down into your opponent's court.

LOB

The lob calls for exquisite control and racket preparation. We'll talk first about the defensive lob, when you are just trying somehow or other to stay in the point. There are

two key elements to the defensive lob. The first is to try to get the lob to your opponent's backhand side. Nobody likes hitting a backhand overhead. The second is to get it high and deep. As I said before, most overhead errors are timing mistakes, and timing the high lob is very difficult. And if your opponent decides to play safe and let the ball bounce before hitting it, you will have backed him up and given yourself some time to recover.

The key to the defensive lob is to really extend your follow-through. Remember, the racket is your tram-

The key to both the offensive lob (shown here) and the defensive lob is to really extend your follow-through.

poline in many ways, and the longer you hold the ball on your strings, the more control you will have.

The offensive lob can be hit in two situations, one more common than the other. The less common shot is used as a means of breaking up your opponent's tempo during a baseline rally. Just take the pace off his shot by lifting back a moonball. Hitting hot does not mean always hitting hard. A lob-type shot to break up a ground-stroke exchange can throw your opponent off stride, especially when it is carried deep and high to his backhand. The more common use of the offensive lob is as a passing shot off a weak volley. In this case, disguise is of the essence. Bring the racket back and turn your shoulders just as you would for a regular ground stroke. Then snap your stroke up, roll your wrist, and brush up the back of the ball more than you would on a defensive lob. Try for a combination of height and topspin. The topspin lob looks a lot like a topspin ground stroke, in terms of the swing. The difference is that with the lob your follow-through is extended higher.

There are several drills encompassing both the lob and overhead that can be practiced in groups of up to six. For four players, divide into two teams, net players versus baseline players. The net players can go no farther back than the service line, and the baseliners try to keep a rally going over them. The baseliners score every time they maintain a lob rally of six or more shots, and the netmen score each time they intercept and put away an overhead.

DAY FIVE:

VOLLEY

I've always liked to volley, but my early training empha-sized ground strokes. The club in Czechoslovakia, like most clubs in Europe, had only soft, clay courts. We were practical students, so we learned the European game, the clay court baseline game. With players like Bjorn Borg dominating men's tennis at that time, there seemed little reason to learn anything else. But the volley has always come naturally to me.

One of the greatest mistakes students make is to take too long a backswing on the volley. Occasionally this will work, and it seems impressive; but it is a low-percent-age shot. One of the keys to the volley is to cut down on that big swing and instead punch through the ball with a compact and controlled stroke. When you are at net, keep the racket head up and out in front of you. If you let the racket head drop below your hand, you are more likely to net the ball as it is more difficult to generate pace.

I use my backhand (continental) grip on both the forehand and the backhand volley. I try to meet the ball as far out in front as possible, letting my shoulders fall forward to ensure that I don't meet the ball late. I punch with a firm motion, for the most part not coming under the ball and slicing, but instead driving through the ball. If you open

VOLLEY

On the volley, cut down on the backswing and punch through the ball with a compact and controlled stroke.

your racket face only slightly on the volley, you'll get the spin and control you need.

Both the forehand and the backhand volley require short, abbreviated, punching strokes. Drive your volleys deep, unless you have the angle to slide them off the side of the court. The volley is not really effective without firm

On the backhand volley you need a firm wrist. Keep the racket head up as you hit through the ball.

control, and for control you need a firm wrist and a properly raised racket head. A firm wrist will prevent you from making weak, blocked volleys. If your wrist is limp, chances are the opponent's pace will dictate your shot. Try to keep the racket head above your wrist at all times. This is obviously impossible on a volley that comes in

around your ankles, but the point is that you need to bend your knees and put your whole body into the volley. More important than the power this drive provides is the control it allows. If you drop the racket head and try to scoop up the low volley, you get only your wrist and your arm into the shot.

Another important shot is the half-volley. This is the shot you're often forced to make when the ball comes back very low. It should be practiced, but it's *not* a shot that you want to hit if you can avoid it, since it's one of the most difficult shots to execute.

HALF-VOLLEY

The key to the half-volley is to get your knees bent and meet the ball out in front of you.

Make the half-volley part of your practice routine by setting up near the service line and having your partner feed you several low-clearance shots that bounce around your feet. The key to the half-volley is getting your knees down and meeting the ball out in front. If you don't do this, the ball will play you, either coming in so low that you can't pick it up, or in so tight to your body that all you can do is pop the ball back up. Don't take a backswing on the half-volley as you're moving in. Your follow-through should be similar to that of a flat ground stroke, carrying the ball just over the net. If you pop the ball up too much, you'll lose the advantage of being at net.

As you finish the half-volley, resist the temptation to pick up your head quickly to see where the ball's gone. Complete the follow-through, then come in to net, waiting on the balls of your feet for that volley you can put away.

That's Day Five. The volley is a vital weapon, and should be practiced thoroughly so that you feel comfortable with it on both the forehand and the backhand.

DAY SIX:

SINGLES AND DOUBLES STRATEGY

Having reviewed the basic strokes of hitting hot, we are ready now to go on to singles strategy. I hope that in the first five days you've given some serious thought to your game, including asking yourself how you can improve your strokes.

SINGLES STRATEGY

Today I want to lay out my ideal singles strategy, the essence of hitting hot. In 1982, I had one of my best years. But I had a very different game from the one I now possess. I rarely came to net, and I relied almost exclusively on wearing down my opponents on the baseline. While I still rely on my ground strokes, I've broadened my game. The game of tennis today is a power game, and it demands that you use all the strokes. It's a combination of baseline consistency and net-play power. This is the singles strategy of hitting hot.

Perhaps the best way to explain this is by answering the question I am most often asked: "What was your greatest match?" I've played so many that seemed crucial at the time that this is difficult to answer, but up to now I would say that the final of the U.S. Open in 1985 would have to be number one. It also happens to be an excellent example of what I consider good singles strategy. I combined the three essentials of any game plan—shot selection, percentage tennis, and playing my opponent's weaknesses—to come up with a way to beat McEnroe.

Essentially, I went into the game thinking that I would hit the ball as hard as I could, coming to net whenever he gave me a short ball. I knew that he'd had a tough five-setter the night before against Mats Wilander, and that he would therefore have a hard time keeping up with a blistering pace. In a way, I was like the heavyweight champion looking to knock out an opponent in the first three rounds.

I started hitting the ball very well, but I was just missing on several key shots. McEnroe was up 3–love, and then 5–2. And yet I was hitting the ball quite well.

At this point I was faced with a crucial decision: either change my game plan or try to weather this storm and go on as planned. I felt strong, so I decided to go for it, especially with my serve coming up. I held serve, and then I broke John in a very tough game. My decision to continue hitting hot had been correct.

You see, my strategy against McEnroe was based on solid propositions. Let's take a look at how I considered the three aspects of putting together a game plan.

1. *Shot selection.* As I said, all tournament long I

had been hitting well. I felt at the top of my game, and knew that I could set the tempo of the match. So I decided to play the power game. I came in on my serve as often as I could, winning 41 of 47 points on my first serve. On my second serve I stayed back a bit more, confident that I could force John into giving me short shots that would lead me into the net. From the baseline, I mixed things up. I tried to keep him on the run, and I used my slice backhand approach often, especially going down the line. Since John was a bit tired, he was reaching for these shots and hitting up to me, giving me the edge at the net. I decided to do all of this on the basis of what had been working well for me before, what looked good in practice, and what I thought would work against John. So, go into the match knowing your shot selection.

2. *Percentage tennis.* Before any match you have to decide, taking into account how well you've been playing and what you need to do against a given opponent, just how aggressive you are going to be. Hitting hot is not necessarily low-percentage, or risky, tennis. When I went into that final against McEnroe, my game plan was high-percentage, considering how well I'd been hitting at the time. A low-percentage decision would have been to go with something entirely outside my normal pattern of play.

There are times when you need an unconventional plan, however. A brilliant example of this strategy was the game plan Arthur Ashe used in his 1975 Wimbledon triumph over Jimmy Connors. Connors was dominating men's tennis at the time, and no one gave Arthur a chance. But Arthur mixed up drop shots, slices, dinks, and serves right into Jimmy's body and threw Jimmy for a loop. He had to generate all the pace himself, and he didn't really know what to do with all the junk Arthur threw at him.

So decide before the game what shots have been working most for you recently. Emphasize these, but always give yourself room for error. While I may have been hitting hot that Sunday afternoon in September 1985, I didn't do anything flashy. I tried to keep the ball a couple of feet inside the lines, moving McEnroe around until I found the opening for a putaway.

3. *Playing your opponent's strengths and weaknesses.* John McEnroe does not have many weaknesses. He has the most remarkable touch of anyone in tennis, a serve that can pull you off the court or nail you down the middle, and great movement on his ground strokes and volleys. I came up with a strategy to move him around and to play the game at an overwhelming pace. But I also used some of what are commonly considered John's strengths against him.

For instance, I was often able to turn that wide swinging serve to my advantage. Since my ground strokes were good and his movement slowed, my anticipation in returning John's wide serve put me in a position to drive the ball down the line past him. Another of John's strengths is his touch on drop and angle volleys. But I was hitting the ball very hard and any time John gave an indication of making that sort of shot, I anticipated and moved in to take the short ball. So one way to attack your opponent is to know his strengths so well that you can turn them to your advantage.

More often, however, you will be attacking your opponent's weaknesses. Martina Navratilova's domination of Chris Evert Lloyd, for instance, depends in great part on the fact that Chris hates to come to the net. When McEnroe was having success against me in 1983 and 1984, he took advantage of the fact that I was not timing my backhand well in those days. Look carefully at your opponent's game, and if you find a weakness, attack it relentlessly.

One final consideration about singles strategy: I am a great believer in that old adage "Change a losing game, stay with a winning one." Don't experiment with new things if you are way out in front. I have seen many players lose matches they considered won, because they got so overconfident that they thought they could experiment a bit. On the other hand, I have seen many players go down without trying any strategy besides the one that's getting them creamed in the first place. There are times in the match when you have to ask yourself if there isn't a better way. Game plans should be solid but not static; don't be afraid to change. Of course, if you're losing but you're still sure that your game is right, as I was at 2–5 down against MacEnroe, then stay with it.

DOUBLES STRATEGY

Doubles strategy is like singles strategy in some ways and quite different in others. I like the game, but singles is both more enjoyable and more important to me. Nevertheless, doubles is a fascinating game, especially from the point of view of strategy, and it can be useful practice for singles play.

The hitting hot game, with its unrelenting pressure, is perfectly suited to doubles. Again, the three basics of singles strategy apply: shot selection, percentage tennis, and playing the opponents' weaknesses.

With respect to positioning, the key is to cover the net, getting there whenever and however you can. But given this basic and universal premise, let's take a look at the details of doubles positioning.

Doubles partners too often make the mistake of dividing the court between them, down the center line. The idea, I guess, is that as long as each guy covers his side, everything will be fine. This just isn't so. Good doubles teams learn to move together. This is why a pair like Ken Flach and Robert Seguso, two fair singles players, can become an awesome doubles team.

When at net, your positioning should take into account two things: where your opponents are and where your partner is. In general, the two of you should shade over to the side of the court that your opponents are hitting from. If your partner moves over to cover the alley, don't be caught covering your side of the court. Slide over to the middle, leaving your opponents only the lob and the small slice of court from which you just moved. You have to give *something* at the net, and it's better to give the tough angles than to give up the entire middle of the court. Just as you move side to side together, you should move up and down the court together. Try to avoid the common mistake of playing one back, one up. You win doubles at the net, together.

Your doubles shot selection should be high-percentage, even though the game lends itself more to lots of putaways. For instance, many baseliners think that every ground stroke they hit has to be a passing shot down the alley. Especially if you have a weak ball to work

When playing doubles, try to move up and down the court with your partner and dominate the net whenever you can. Don't just divide the court between you down the center line but move together in the direction of play.

with, try to set up your opponents by nailing a sharp ground stroke down the middle from time to time. Mix up your passes, keeping the other team off balance with a combination of lobs, down-the-line passing shots, and groundies up the middle. At net, it's important to develop a good angle volley. While most of your volleys are going to be hit deep, your putaway volleys will need to be angled off to the side, away from the two players covering the baseline.

As in singles, attack your opponents' weaknesses. Returning serve is the greatest weakness in doubles, so develop a good spin serve that will drive the receiver deep with a strong kick. Keeping that first serve deep and consistent is the key to maintaining your service edge. If you use a hard, flat, and inconsistent serve, your opponents will have more opportunities to attack your second serve and even things up.

One final word about doubles. Enjoy yourself. You have another person out there on your side. If you're getting tense, or you have some gripe with him, talk it out. Good doubles teams speak both silently and verbally. They communicate with hand signals, and they plot out their strategy by talking throughout the match. Don't lose a doubles match for mental reasons, especially when you respect your partner as a person and as a tennis player. Talk with your partner; you're a team out there, both mentally and physically.

DAY SEVEN:

STATION DRILLS

There are two ways to learn tennis. The first is through playing, and the second is through practice. Both aspects are crucial, and if you neglect either, your game is bound to suffer. Today I want to list several station drills that can be helpful tools for improving your strokes. Station drills may not be very exciting, but they improve your game immensely.

GROUND STROKES

1. For two players, one of the best drills for placement and control is to rally in an alley. This is not a competitive drill. Both players try to keep a rally going in the alley for as long as they can. All shots must land behind the service line. Switch sides of the alley from time to time, thus developing crosscourt rallies of forehand to forehand and

backhand to backhand, as well as forehand to backhand down the line.

2. Another competitive drill for two players is to play a game to 21, using only half the court, so that both players are hitting either crosscourt at the same time or down the line at the same time. Points are scored when balls land either beyond the baseline or inside the service line. Each player must hit one ground stroke in before the ball is considered in play.

3. A competitive drill for five players is the Figure Eight rally. Four players hit in a figure eight pattern, with a player on the sideline ready to fill in. Each player starts with two balls. If he misses a shot he must start the next rally with one ball, and if he misses again, he starts with no balls. One more mistake, and he goes to the sideline, where he jumps rope while the fifth player fills in.

SERVE AND RETURN

1. There are several good serve-and-return drills, but my favorite was designed by my coach, Tony Roche. The server serves from the service line or from halfway between the service line and the baseline. He serves ten balls. The returner, at the baseline or a foot behind, gets a point every time he returns one of those serves. The server scores every time the receiver misses. Clearly, the receiver is overchallenged with the server in so close. But he gets great practice in handling powerful serves while at the same time conditioning his reflexes and timing on the chip return.

Net drills sharpen your reflexes and shorten your backswing on the volley.

VOLLEY AND OVERHEAD

1. There are many, many ways to practice the volley. This particular drill works on your reactions at the net. One feeder stands opposite two players at net. The netmen are both in ready position, and the feeder hits a series of balls without any particular order. The netmen volley back anything that comes near them. Three volley misses and you're out. The remaining player becomes the feeder for the next round.

2. Many people have a difficult time handling powerful shots at net, especially after a strong rush forward. This drill is designed to combine the approach with a series of difficult high-speed volleys. The feeder should have six balls at hand. The drilling player comes forward with an approach shot and then comes to net. The feeder should not worry about where the player's shots land but instead should fire off the next shot immediately after the incoming player hits the previous one. At net the player receives one ball hard to the forehand, one ball hard to the back-

hand, and one ball hard right at him. The feeder should hit so hard that any backswing on the netman's part will result in an error. The final ball, a reward of sorts, should be a deep lob, sending the opponent back toward the baseline. This last shot is something of a relief, but it also gives the player a chance to work on a good scissors kick to get up to that high lob as he moves backward.

MOVEMENT

On-court movement is a series of sprints and lateral movements that aren't developed in long-distance running. Good footwork can be developed through constant and well-directed practice.

1. A grueling exercise is the Davis Cup drill, also known as the Kamikaze. (And I'm sure there are lots of less flattering names for this.) A feeder stands at net with approximately thirty balls. He feeds them one by one to the player at the baseline, moving the balls around the whole court. The feeder should release each ball at just about the time that the player makes contact with the previous one. The player's aim is to run down every shot on the first bounce, while also working on getting every shot over the net. This can be a good drill if the feeder mixes up the balls well, bringing the player up and back and moving him from side to side. You learn quickly that an exaggerated backswing makes meeting the ball out in front a difficult task on every ball you have to chase down. You also learn what sort of shape you're in!

2. Another good movement drill is running the lines. Starting at the baseline, run up the outside doubles line, run backward down the alley line to the service line, shuf-

fle to the center service line, run forward to the net and then backward again to the "T," shuffle to the other alley, run up again to the net, then backward down the outside alley, and shuffle across to where you started. This is a fun way to end a practice. If you're among a large group, you can turn it into an all-out relay race. And, of course, it covers the three types of tennis movement: sideways, forward, and backward.

DAY EIGHT:
APPROACH SHOT

The approach shot requires a cool head. In their hurry to get to the net many players forget the fundamentals. In so doing, they tend to rush their shots, losing control and depth on their approaches. Remember that an approach shot is not meant to hit a winner but simply to get you into position at the net so as to finish the point.

I will discuss the forehand approach shot only briefly, for it seems to me a far easier shot than the backhand. As you approach on the forehand, the first thing to do is turn your shoulders. In most cases you will be moving in on a short ball, and it is best to meet the ball early and out in front, taking it on the rise so that you use the momentum of your opponent's shot to generate power and depth. Come up the back of the ball and extend your follow-through deep.

Some people believe you have to come in, stop, set up, and then hit the approach shot. That's fine, but it can disrupt the tempo of your shot. It also delays your movement into the net. I try to move through my forehand approach, trusting that the short backswing and the top-spin will keep the ball from flying long. You must keep your head down throughout the shot, however. The temptation to look up quickly is great, but any head movement will pull your swing and your knees up too quickly.

The backhand slice keeps the ball low, forcing your opponent to hit up to you at the net. It also gives you superb control and good depth, thereby giving you the opportunity to cut off your opponent's angles at the net.

To hit the backhand slice approach, take a high backswing, turn your shoulders, and cock the wrist of your racket hand. Leaning into the ball as if your shoulder was trying to knock down a barn door, swing through the ball, coming under it as you come forward. Try to keep the shoulders closed. The shoulders will hide whether you are planning to hit down the line or crosscourt. Finish the slice by coming up again with the racket head, extending your follow-through forward for depth. Resist the temptation to come up too quickly with your head. The backhand slice approach, when hit well, has you leaning forward into the shot, and this leads nicely into a run to the net.

So much for the mechanics of the approach shot. We will get more involved in the placement and strategy of coming to net on Day Eleven. An entire day may seem a lot to devote to the approach shot, but it's a vitally important part of the game and should be practiced thoroughly.

On the approach shot, whether forehand or backhand (shown here), the key is to keep your head down throughout the stroke and move forward as you follow through so that you can get to net.

DAY NINE:

SERVE AND VOLLEY

I've always been able to put opponents on the defensive by combining power and placement on my serve to set up the rest of the point. But until recently I took advantage of this edge only from the baseline, and if my opponent came up with a good return, we would then be on equal terms, battling out a baseline rally. But then Tony Roche and I started working on my volley. And as that improved, I started following my serve to the net, adding a whole new dimension to my game.

Let me caution you, however. Having a good serve and a good volley is not enough. You need to put the two together into one fluid motion. In this chapter we will look at the serve and volley as one continuous movement.

The first thing to do is to toss the ball out in front without sacrificing height. Many players stretch themselves forward in an effort to hurry their way to the net, while tossing the ball so low that they greatly lessen their chances of getting any kick on the serve. Second, stretch out completely in an effort to meet the toss at its peak. Thus, you will start with all your energy flowing up and out, giving power and spin to the ball at the same time as you fling yourself toward the net.

The next thing is land on the balls of your feet rather than flat-footed. This means that you are balanced and ready to push off as soon as you land, making the rush to the net a fluid part of the serve rather than a new and separate motion.

Glide into the net. Move fast, so that it seems your feet barely touch the ground. When you do stop to set up for a low volley, you are still leaning in toward the net, your weight going forward.

After your first volley, follow the flight of your shot as you go in toward the net. If you've angled the shot toward the side of the court, you'll cut off the down-the-line shot while leaving little room for the crosscourt angle shot. Close in on the net as far as you can, and volley into the space created by your first volley. The closer you are to the net, the more angles you'll give yourself. Be prepared for the lob, though, if you're opponent has the time to make it.

Service placement and pace are crucial to the serve and volley. McEnroe's serve and volley can be devastating when his wide-swinging serve is working well. By pulling your opponent out of the court, you make the task of following your serve to the net much easier. There are only two effective replies to a wide-swinging serve: the sharp crosscourt, which has to be hit so that it drops in the upper far corner of the opposite service box; and the deep shot down the line that catches the corner just

inside the baseline. But these are low-percentage shots. And by following your wide serve to within a couple of feet of the alley, you will have cut off all other possible angles.

Another possible placement of the serve to set up a volley is right at your opponent. This works especially well against opponents who use angles to their advantage. In this case, you want to follow the path of the serve, perhaps setting yourself up a bit farther back than you normally would. Chances are your opponent will pop the ball back weakly, and you'll be able to move *in* as well as *over* to the ball.

When you serve and volley, the important thing is to be balanced on the balls of your feet as your opponent hits his return. Then you can move in beyond the service line to make your first volley.

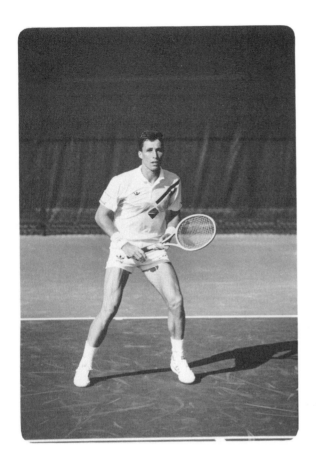 

Mix up your placement of both serve and volley. If your opponent knows just what sort of serve you're hitting, or just where all your volleys are going, you'll eventually start getting passed. Also, be sure that you mix up the serve and volley with a baseline game. No matter how strong your power game, the bit of variety that keeps your opponent guessing will pay off in the long run.

DAY TEN:

SERVING AND
RECEIVING POSITIONS

Tennis is a game with a long history, and most of the traditions are in place for good reasons. But not all. I don't think learning tennis means simply accepting traditional ways of playing the game. Each great new player brings something new to the game: Connors and the intensity behind that two-handed backhand; Borg and the revolution of topspin; McEnroe with the unprecedented serving stance and unbelievable touch. These are just a few of the additions to the game of tennis that would never have happened if these players had been bound by tradition.

I believe that we are once again changing the course of tennis. Hitting hot is relentless, athletic tennis, the like of which has never been seen before. Its demands are unprecedented: complete athletic and mental determination, combined with a realistic blend of low- and high-risk pressure.

When Tony Roche and I went about restructuring

my game in an effort to make it more complete, I was determined but a bit wary. After all, I was one of the top three players in the world, with a game that I'd worked on for almost twenty years. Why risk tampering with something that good? But as we kept working, I realized that it was possible to try to develop a game that had no outstanding weaknesses. The key to eventual improvement was that we believed it could actually happen, and Tony and I were willing to put in the hard work.

If you are really interested in developing your game, you will have to make the same sort of effort. Don't be afraid to try something that runs against the grain of most teaching. If it works for you, then it's right for your game whether others agree with you or not.

SERVING

Serving and receiving positions involve traditions that you might want to tamper with a bit. The old saw is that you serve from just next to the center line, you return from about a foot inside the alley lines and a couple of feet behind the baseline, and you stand on the service line when your partner is receiving in doubles.

When I serve from the deuce court, I stand a foot or two from the center line. This gives me a great angle down the middle, over the lowest part of the net, to a right-handed opponent's backhand. I also feel comfortable in that position if I want to swing the ball wide and come in to the net.

When I serve from the ad court, I shift over a couple of feet farther from the center line. This gives me a better angle at the backhand corner but doesn't take me

When serving from the ad court, I shift over a couple of feet from the center line so as to create some angles for myself.

so far over that I'm vulnerable to the return down the line. For doubles, my serving position is a little wider, with some variation depending on what I'm trying to do with the first serve.

RECEIVING

The receiving position is dictated to a great extent by your opponent's serve. I often start out a couple of feet behind the spot where I intend to meet the ball. Then, as the server tosses the ball, I move in, so that when I meet the ball my weight is moving forward. In the deuce court I usually start out about halfway between the center line and the outside alley, while in the ad court I'm usually farther over toward the alley. In both cases I'm trying to get the server to go to my strongest side, the forehand.

Many players don't use the receiving position as forcefully as they should, especially on the second serve.

When receiving in the ad court, I stand over toward the alley, trying to get the server to go to my stronger side, the forehand.

The second serve is your opportunity to take the initiative. I usually try to take a weak second serve on my forehand. Start off in your customary receiving position, but as the server tosses, move over toward the backhand side. This will open up your forehand without presenting too much of a problem if the server comes in to your backhand side. By starting out a couple of feet behind your intended contact point, you will be throwing yourself into the return with the force necessary for a good approach.

When your partner is serving in doubles, your position at the net will generally depend on what the two of you have decided to do with the serve. Generally, however, a safe guideline is to position yourself halfway between the outside alley line and the center line.

When your partner is returning serve, don't be afraid to move in about halfway between the service line and the net. Doubles is won on the offensive; and you should always be looking to move in.

DAY ELEVEN:
COMING TO NET

From here on we will get more and more specific as we try to round out your game. We will cover specific game situations as well as pregame rituals and preparation for tournaments.

I am often asked if there was any one time when I knew, absolutely knew, that I would be a world champion in this sport. The answer is no. I have, however, had several moments when I realized my game would step up another level. One of these occurred after the 1984 French Open, when I won my first Grand Slam tournament, and another after the 1985 U.S. Open final.

In between those times, however, came a lot of doubt, a lot of uncertainty about my future in tennis. This sort of thing never goes away. Tennis isolates you psychologically. No matter how supportive your friends and family might be, you are always out there on your own. It's not like football or soccer, where the coach can always send in a sub. (And believe me, there have been times when I've looked over to Tony, wishing that he could send someone in. Everyone has bad days.)

At this point in the clinic, I want you to think about your attitude toward the game of tennis. Why do you keep practicing so hard? Where is this practice leading you? Is the pressure you feel to improve positive or negative? You see, I think it's very important to remember that tennis is just a game—a beautiful, exciting game, to be sure, but nevertheless a game, something to be enjoyed and not suffered. Keeping a good perspective on that can help you to ride out the moments of self-doubt.

I'm not going to tell you that you have to come to net all the time. I'm not even going to tell you that you have to come to net at all. You create your own game. I am, however, going to insist that it is impossible to play the complete pressure tennis that is dominating the tennis world today if you don't come to net. Coming to net, and doing so successfully, establishes you as an aggressive opponent.

The very term "rushing the net" implies a certain recklessness. There's nothing wrong with conveying recklessness. It can make your opponent wary. But there's a great difference between appearing reckless and being reckless.

When Boris Becker rushes the net, he may seem out of control, but actually he is on the balls of his feet, ready to go in any direction. I think the key to control while coming to net is the first volley. If you are so anxious to get to the net that you run through that first volley, or you are caught hitting a half-volley, chances are that you will hit a poor shot, and also that you will reach the net without having really considered your positioning. Getting to net quickly does you no good if that first volley is poor. So take your time. Come off the serve or approach with a definite idea of how far inside the service line you want to get. Come to a stop, however brief, on the balls of your feet (this is called split step), feet apart at shoulder width. Try to get that first volley deep, with the idea of forcing your opponent to pop up a weak return. Unless you have an easy, high ball, use that first volley more as a set-up shot than as a pure winner. Then, as I've said before, close in on the net as far as you can. Even if your opponent has a fine lob, your good approach volley makes closing in tight a worthwhile gamble.

Many players attack the net in the same manner every time. They drive their approach shot deep to their opponent's backhand time after time, whether it works or not, because that's what one is "supposed to do" on the approach shot. Of course you should stay with a winning game. And if you're rushing the net successfully by attacking the backhand repeatedly, fine. But in general, I think players should try to mix up their approach shots, for two reasons. The first has to do with position. If your opponent knows that you are going to hit to his backhand, he's going to start sneaking over that way, and before you know it he'll be in a groove, passing you and lobbing with ease. Keep him guessing by swinging wide and sometimes hitting short balls over to his forehand. The second reason is psychological. If you attack someone's backhand enough, chances are he'll get accustomed to that shot and start to hit his backhand pass consistently well.

*If you have placed your
first volley well, you will
be able to dominate
the net on your second
and put the ball away.*

But if you keep him off balance by mixing up your approaches, your net game will become all the more overpowering. By winning points from both his backhand and his forehand, you are affirming the sort of total dominance that can shock even a potentially better player into submission.

And this, finally, is the last reason for developing a strong net game. Net play can be the joker in any match, the equalizer that brings a weaker player up to the level of a player whose overall game is more consistent. Kevin Curren, Steve Denton, and Roscoe Tanner are just a few of the players who can win a match on the strength of their net games alone.

That's Day Eleven. Practice coming to net in two stages, using a first volley that opens up the court, and a second that finishes the point. And practice it repeatedly.

DAY TWELVE:

DROP SHOT

AND DROP VOLLEY

In this chapter I'd like to discuss the drop shot and the drop volley. It's shots like these that will round out your game and make it difficult for an opponent to peg you as a certain type of player. Both shots are useful, both as putaways and as shots that keep your opponent off balance.

The drop shot can really wreak havoc on an opponent's game plan. If that game plan is built around establishing a consistent and powerful backcourt game, it's important that you mix up your shots to keep him from getting in any sort of groove. A couple of drop shots early on in a match will keep him off balance.

Hitting the drop shot demands great touch and great disguise. Turn your shoulders and bring the racket

**DROP
SHOT**

On both the drop shot and the drop volley, hold the racket head very flat, as shown here. Come under the ball and lift the racket a bit.

back in *exactly* the manner you would for a regular ground stroke. For instance, on my forehand my racket face is closed until the last moment, even though eventually I will come under the ball. You must keep your opponent guessing on the drop shot. If not, he'll anticipate it and move in to pick it up.

As you stroke the drop shot, come under the ball and finish with a gentle lift. Many players slash down at their drop shot, hoping to generate a wicked slice that will kill any bounce. More important than killing the bounce is controlling the shot, being able to place it short and to the side farthest from your opponent. By coming under the ball and then lifting a bit, you generate underspin while at the same time controlling the ball with that little bit of body movement you bring into the shot.

One final word on the drop shot. Unless you have an excellent one, use the drop shot primarily off a short ball. A drop shot hit from the baseline is a very low percentage shot.

The drop volley can be an excellent controlled putaway when you are closing in on the net. Rather than creating your own power by punching through the ball and keeping your wrist firm, you work this volley off your opponent's pace. Collect the ball onto your racket by giving with the wrist. Then use just a light forward motion with the wrist and forearm to place the ball. All the power you need will be derived from your opponent's shot, and the placement you want will come from the wrist motion as well as the shoulder turn in the intended direction.

That's Day Twelve. These are the classy shots, shots that will give you many more options in matches and will persuade your opponent that you are a force to be reckoned with. But they need a great deal of practice before they can become effective.

DROP VOLLEY

DAY THIRTEEN:

BASELINE RALLIES

Most of the top players today have clearly defined games. Connors is a relentless baseliner who wins through constant pressure. McEnroe relies on extraordinary touch and intuition. Kevin Curren is a serve-and-volley player. All these players understand what their strengths are, and they do all they can to reinforce and develop those attributes. While none are tied down to one style of play, they know that when the chips are down they can rely on certain strengths.

It takes a long time to recognize and develop all your strengths. For a time I relied almost exclusively on my serve and forehand, and for a time that strategy worked. But as opponents grew used to that strategy, those strengths turned into a kind of weakness, as opponents exploited the other parts of my game. So I had to develop a broader strategy, the one I now call hitting hot. It took some time, but Tony Roche and I finally reworked my game so that I can now rely on strokes that I once used to neglect, such as my net play. Try to develop a variety of patterns in your own game, patterns that you can rely on at any time.

Once these patterns have been developed, there are many ways to maintain them. Establishing various routines can be an important boost to your game. One example of this is my preservice routine. I always bounce the ball three times before my first serve and four before the second. I try to take time before each serve, even when I am hitting hot and am in complete control of the match. Before each point I give myself a few moments when I can analyze my strokes and strategy thus far, or consider what I'm going to try to do on the upcoming point.

Try to establish patterns that emphasize your strengths. Then try to reinforce these patterns with routines that fit into the flow of your game.

Baseline rallies are the foundation of my game. I try to set the tone of the match from the baseline, I try to analyze my opponent's weaknesses from the baseline, and I try to wear my opponent out from the baseline.

Baseline rallies depend on patterns. Going into a match, you should decide what you want to do from the baseline. Are you going to try to run your opponent around? Are you going to attack his backhand? Will you use the baseline rallies only to set up your net game?

All these questions need to be considered before you get out to the court. The first few games of the match should be used to establish your chosen pattern. If it

Baseline rallies are the foundation of my game. And good racket preparation is essential if you are to keep a rally going.

works, stay with it. If not, be prepared to switch to a second pattern.

Another important point to remember in baseline rallies is the idea of mixing your shots up. Too often baseliners hit in one set way, whether using moonballs, low-clearance flat shots, or just slice backhands and topspin forehands. While you do want to emphasize your strengths, you also want to throw your opponent off stride. Throw in a slice to the service line with a deep topspin to the backhand. Move your opponent up and back as well as from side to side. You should use the baseline rally to establish your own pattern while undermining your opponent's.

One final point about baseline rallying. Don't go for the lines. Even at the top of the professional ranks, most points are won off errors. Sure, there's the occasional brilliant victory, when the winner nails all the lines and serves thirty aces. Those wins are hard to ignore; they are the matches people remember. But overall consistency is the name of the game.

When I want to move my opponent around on the baseline, I try to keep the ball two to four feet inside the lines. Aiming for spots closer to the lines just doesn't make sense. Your percentages drop drastically, and the foot or so farther that your opponent has to run isn't worth the risk. Set up your putaways by moving your opponent around for several shots. Eventually he will get tired, opening up a section of the court, or he'll give you a short ball that you can attack. So remember, patience pays, especially at the baseline, where consistency is the name of the game. And there's no better way to establish consistency than to practice your ground strokes until hitting from the baseline seems like second nature.

DAY FOURTEEN:
MORE STATION DRILLS

I have never stopped learning. Tennis constantly presents new challenges, both mental and physical.

If I had not become a tennis player, I probably would have gotten involved in computers or mathematics in some way. Both subjects are unlimited, offering possibilities that stretched far beyond my abilities as a student. But it seemed to me that each subject could be mastered in small chunks. If I worked hard enough and long enough at a certain type of problem, eventually I would get it. And after that, I could move on to the next problem. I might never solve everything, but at least I would be moving in the right direction.

Tennis offers the same chances for improvement through trial and error. Mentally, this was made clear for me as I tried to overcome the label of "choker" in big matches. I never thought the label was justified, but it is true that I played better when I wasn't the favorite.

After a lot of questioning and some disappointing losses, I realized that you can eliminate the fear of losing and start concentrating on winning. One of the ways to do this is to imagine that you have lost already. Then you have nothing more to lose and you live through that fear. When you get out on the court, you say "This is only an exercise," and you relax.

One of the improvements in my game has come about through a better understanding of court angles. I used to approach the net almost exclusively down the line. In fact, I was so repetitive that opponents started to cheat over to the line when they saw me coming to net, and even though that gave me an easy crosscourt shot, I more often than not opted to go down the line. This was how I had been taught. And I dare say it's how the approach is still taught.

The lesson I eventually learned is fairly simple. By approaching crosscourt, you clear the lowest part of the net and you give yourself more court to hit into. This shot, if not a winner, should at least put your opponent in such a position that he has to hit up to you at the net. Finally, by pulling your opponent wide with the crosscourt approach you open the whole court for a crosscourt putaway volley. And remember, we've been talking all along about closing in on the net. Close in after your approach and look for that sharp angle volley.

APPROACH SHOT

Station drills involving the approach shot are easy to set up. This one involves three players, one feeding and two at the opposite baseline, taking turns. The feeder delivers a short ball to the first player, who hits a forehand approach shot crosscourt. The feeder returns a reachable shot down the line and the approaching player tries to put it away crosscourt. If he fails, the two players play out the point. The second player follows and does the same thing. Then the drill is repeated with down-the-line approach shots, and finally with down-the-line and crosscourt approaches off the backhand. Remember, the backhand slice can be a very effective approach shot, especially when you hit a good angled crosscourt, keeping the ball low and skidding off the court.

MOVEMENT

I have spent lots of time working on my footwork. I suggested a couple of movement drills earlier, and I'd like to highlight another one here. Court movement involves more than just getting to the ball. It also involves getting back into position. This drill is run as a timed competition among five players. Four players stand at stations, all on the same side of the net, one at each end of the baseline, one at each side corner of the service boxes. The fifth player stands at the center of the baseline on the same side of the net as the other players. An instructor assigns a number to each of the stations, and then calls out one of these numbers. The player whose number has been called drops a ball out in front of him, and the fifth, or hitting, player runs to that position, strokes the ball, and then returns to his ready position at the baseline. Then the instructor calls another number and the drill is repeated. Each of the players at the stations has two balls.

Once the player has hit all eight balls and has returned to his ready position, he is finished. Players are penalized seconds for balls missed. This drill emphasizes total court movement while focusing the player's attention on stroking the ball on the run.

RETURN OF SERVE

I believe in practicing the return of serve as an overchallenge. The Tony Roche drill, which we discussed earlier, does this. So does the following drill, designed for chip returns with little or no backswing. The server follows his serve into the service line and stands ready there. If the receiver can chip the ball past him, the point is the receiver's. If the server can get that first volley back without moving from his position, the point goes to the server. The receiver should be able to win pretty consistently from a couple of feet behind the baseline. But after ten serves in that position, he should move up to the baseline. This will demand an even shorter backswing of him, and emphasize meeting the ball out in front with a volleylike punch. After a series at this position, the receiver should then move in another three feet. This will be the consummate overchallenge, and the receiver will be at a great disadvantage. But the overchallenge will make real game situations seem easy and will also give the receiver greater confidence when attacking the second serve.

That's Day Fourteen. Practice these station drills with your friends until you've got them down.

This is the last day of my 14-day clinic. But there's more to come! The following chapters describe those other aspects of the game that you should think about all the time.

PRACTICING

It may seem strange to have a separate chapter about practicing. After all, you might say, haven't we done enough of that already? The answer is an unequivocal no. If there is one constant about my tennis life, it is practice. When you first start to play, you practice the basic motions of each shot. Once you're hitting with some understanding of why you stroke the ball the way you do, practice turns those undisciplined muscle motions into muscle memories that you can rely on. Finally, practice and experimentation allow you to develop the touch shots, such as the drop shot and drop volley, the shots that can lift your game out of the ordinary.

The most important sort of practice is the practice you demand of yourself, when you make yourself go out and hit a certain stroke a hundred times, even if you'd rather be at home watching TV. That self-discipline pays dividends in addition to the immediate one of stroke improvement. Players whose practice routines are well established are less likely to break down in difficult match situations. They understand what bearing down is all about.

You should be just as concerned with improvement as you are with winning. And don't forget tournament losses. A couple of days after the end of a tournament, try to reconstruct your matches. What were the high points? What were your best strokes, and what were your worst? Why did one player suffer against your backhand approach while another handled it with ease? How was your footwork? I keep a book on all my opponents and past matches to help me in future matches against those same players.

If you have a coach, the two of you should go over these things together. If not, step back from your game and try to look at it as if you were watching someone else's. This sort of mental discipline can turn bad tournament experiences into useful practice sessions.

You should know how to practice alone as well as with other people. It's always most tempting to get a friend and rally, but there are some important things to be gained from solo practice.

Using the backboard is helpful, both when you are starting out and later on, when you are working on a particular ground stroke. When I was very young I used it all the time. The combination of my age and the limited court supply made it very difficult for me to play with other people, so I took my racket or wooden paddle to the backboard and played there. Find a backboard that's in good shape. Many are cracked or located on an uneven surface. You should use the backboard to groove a stroke, to turn muscle motions into muscle memories. Work on the forehand alone or the backhand alone. Concentrate less on where you're putting the ball on the backboard than on how you're stroking the ball. Use backboard practice to check such specifics of your swing as whether your backswing is under control or not, whether your shoulders are fully turned, and whether your follow-through is properly extended or not. Even advanced players will go to the backboard, using it as a place to check and correct bad habits that may have developed in their strokes from too much playing and not enough practice.

Serving is another thing that can be practiced alone. I am all in favor of the idea of going out and serving a bucket of balls, provided that this practice has some discipline to it. Use targets; the tangible proof of success will make more of an impact than just telling yourself you will hit to one of the corners of the service box. Work on one type of serve at a time. Serve a bucket of flat serves down the middle, then serve a bucket of second serves wide. If you are having trouble getting enough kick on the ball, start with your racket already in the backscratch position. Trying to hit the serve from this position will emphasize the upward snap.

When you practice your ground strokes with another player, it's important again to establish a certain framework. After getting warmed up, start hitting corner to corner. Concentrate on keeping the ball deep and on establishing a groove. Use the whole court; this is your highest-percentage shot, over the low part of the net and with the longest stretch of the court to hit into, so you should take advantage of it. Go forehand to forehand and backhand to backhand, giving equal time to each stroke. After just drilling for some time, you can play a corner-to-corner game. Make four deep shots and then play out a point, coming to net on any shot that bounces within the service line.

Another much neglected and useful way to practice with a partner is to volley back and forth. Again, this is a drill that should be done in stages. Start out at the service line. Don't try to force your opponent into bad shots. Just return the ball to him. Move in a step every time you have a good rally of twenty or more. As you move in, you will be forced to rely on your quickness and good reactions. Many people think that these qualities must be God-given. I disagree, and volleying back and forth is one way to develop these very necessary skills.

TOURNAMENTS

Every tournament I have entered had something unique about it. Each presented so many different physical and mental pressures that suggesting any one way of handling a tournament is bound to go under the heading of general advice rather than hard-and-fast rules. Nevertheless, I'd like to give some suggestions on tournament preparation, winning strategies, and handling the jitters.

There are several things you can do to prepare for a tournament. Mentally, the first thing to do is relax. There's no reason to get anxious about a tournament. Anxiety gets in the way of clear thinking. The second thing you should do is take a look at your game on the eve of the tournament. What are your strengths? What strokes have you been hitting with particular effectiveness recently? Plan to start the tournament emphasizing your current strengths. Of course, as the tournament goes on you may be forced to change, but you should go into the tournament confident about certain clear strengths.

Once you see the draw, start to analyze the weaknesses of your first opponent. (Of course you'll want to look down the whole draw and imagine where your toughest matches might come. But spending too much time doing this can be fatal. Take one opponent at a time; if you don't, there probably won't be a next one.) The combination of your strengths and your opponent's weaknesses should dictate your game strategies.

As you progress through the tournament, try not to get too anxious about each opponent. Although I usually know my next opponent before I go to bed, I don't worry about the strategy I will use against him till the next day. If I think about strategy too much, I won't get good sleep, and then whatever strategy I've planned won't make any difference anyway. Tournaments are physically demanding. Get lots of sleep, don't smoke, and don't drink. I know there's a great temptation to party when you're away from home at a tournament. There may be a place for that sort of thing in your life. But don't kid yourself. If you party, you'll be in worse shape. You need all your physical resources during a tournament.

In terms of winning strategies, let me reemphasize two things. Your game strategy should be dictated by the best combination of your strengths and your opponent's weaknesses. It should also be dictated by sensible, high-percentage tennis. Saying to yourself "I'm going to come to net on every point" is just not sensible, even if your opponent has weak passing shots and you have a fabulous net game. You have to be prepared to mix things up a bit and to be patient. If you come into the match with only one idea, chances are that by the fourth or fifth game, your opponent will have grooved on your pattern.

Everyone gets nervous about tournaments, both during and before. There are a number of things you can do to combat the jitters. For one, try to keep your life outside the tournament as regular as possible. Eat your usual foods, get your usual sleep, enjoy your usual friends. Keeping things regular helps take off the pressure; you realize that the tournament is not the only thing in life that matters. During matches, there are several things you can do to avoid nervousness. Don't let your mind wander ahead. Keep your concentration on the point at hand. Establish routines: Drink from the same cup on the changeover, bounce the ball the same number of times before each serve, and so forth. These routines will keep you from getting too harried.

If you're losing, change your game plan. But don't do so in a panic. Remember my earlier suggestion. Imagine that you have already lost the match, and that you are trying out a new game plan just for fun. Imagining that, you have nothing more to lose, and you may come up with a rational game plan based on strategy instead of anxiety.

Ask yourself if you're having fun playing tournaments. If not, think about how you can go about trying to achieve a more reasonable balance between competitive pressure and tennis enjoyment. It will help your game, and more important, it may help you feel better about yourself.

CHANNELING PRESSURE

Once upon a time, there were only two countries in the world that played tennis: Australia and America. Oh, sure, France had the "Four Musketeers" in the 1930s, and many other countries produced the occasional good player. But certainly from the 1940s onward, Australia and America dominated the tennis world. The Americans dominated through a combination of sheer numbers and advanced coaching. There seemed to be no end to those champions from California and Florida, raised on a power game that no other country could possibly match.

The Australians, however, stayed with the Americans, even with a much smaller pool of players from which to draw. They did it with great athleticism and the coaching genius of the late Harry Hopman. Hopman produced a slew of brilliant players: Neale Fraser, John Newcombe, Fred Stolle, Rod Laver, Ken Rosewall, Evonne Goolagong and others, including my coach, Tony Roche.

Hopman was willing to experiment. He would try anything to win, while demanding a physical regimen that was far tougher than anything seen in the United States.

This Australian coaching legacy lives on, and its spirit has been adopted in several European countries. Youth development programs in Germany, France, Czechoslovakia, and especially Sweden have given rise to a new generation of European players who are equal to and sometimes better than the best the States has to offer. The United States can no longer rely on numerical superiority to assure tennis supremacy. The best coaching is now available across the Atlantic, and if American tennis doesn't wake up soon, its coaching expertise will soon be hopelessly outdated. The pressure is now on the United States to catch up.

I want to discuss the question of pressure at this point, as it relates to your game. We'll start with the pressure imposed on you by other players and the game itself.

One of the hardest things to do over the course of a series of tournaments is to maintain a positive self-image. Let's face it; most of us are not winning all the time. In fact, there are times when we are losing more often than not. I remember playing in the eighteen-and-unders when I was thirteen. Right in the middle of a match I would throw my hands up in self-disgust. "What am I doing out here?" I would think. "I don't even belong on the same court as the big guys!" And in my frustration I'd hit a terrible shot on the next point, and the opponent would put away an overhead smash, as if to confirm my despair.

In those bad times, it's very important to try to remember what you do well as a tennis player. Take time to remember your strengths. If there's a friend around to talk with, get him to help you out. And try to look at tennis as a long-term project. There are going to be hills and valleys, just as in life, and just as in life, you'll get past the bad times to enjoy better days ahead. So take that self-criticism and turn it into something positive. While it's important to be critical, it's also important to give yourself a lift by occasionally focusing on what you do right.

Losing, especially in tournaments, can put a great deal of pressure on you. After all, there's nothing you can ever do to get that match back. It's gone, lost forever. After a loss, try to forget the score and to concentrate instead on the details of the match. Take a step back from your game. I try to look at the match with the eye of a coach trying to figure out why that fellow Ivan didn't follow through more on his passing shots, why his slice backhand was sitting up rather than skidding off the court, and so on. If you can relax and use losses as a basis for improvement, you'll be able to take a great deal of pressure off yourself.

The motivation for such a critical, healthy look at your game should come from yourself. Before you talk with your coach or others about a losing match, go over the match yourself. I don't believe tennis players respond well to motivation forced on them by outside pressures. In deciding to play serious tennis, after all, you chose a sport with all sorts of built-in pressures, most important the pressure of having no one else to blame for mistakes but yourself. If you enjoy tennis, you thrive on that sort of pressure. But if tennis is something that has been imposed on you, or if it's a sport you've chosen because you want to be well liked, or because you hope to make lots of money, your motivation will not be strong enough to handle pressure well. Any growth or improvement in your game should come about as a result of your own desire. The best reason for trying to improve is that you love the game, and you realize that the better you get, the more you'll enjoy it.

A brief comment about the pressure you exert on your opponents. Just as you want to control your own game mentally, your opponent is looking to control his. I don't believe in trying to psyche out an opponent with wild movements and obnoxious statements. I do think, however, that you can psyche your opponent out by letting him see that you feel completely in control of yourself and of the match. Try not to show your frustration. Any time you see your opponent do so, attack whatever caused the anxiety. Try to be aware of your opponent's moods throughout a match, while keeping your own feelings to yourself. The more you can pressure your opponent's weakness, the less chance he will have to play a level-headed game.

A final comment for younger players about pressure. Everyone has had parental pressure in one form or another. I can't pretend to know everything about all parents, and you alone know just how to deal with and appreciate yours. But I can draw a couple of lessons from my own experience that might be helpful. I think my parents were very good with me as I grew into a tennis life. They presented the game to me as an option, as something they enjoyed greatly and that I might enjoy as well. And once I started playing somewhat seriously, they encouraged me to do my best. Like all families, we had fights along the way. But our fights came about generally when I insisted on hitting one way and they insisted I was doing it wrong. We didn't fight about whether or not I had to go to practice; I wanted to go. I think they understood that I loved the game, and that that love would carry me as far as I wanted to go with the game.

Early on, I relied on them for a great deal of support. But that support gradually shifted as I started relying instead on coaches and friends. My parents were very good in letting me go. For instance, once I beat my mother, we didn't play any more competitive tennis. Instead, we just practiced on my strokes.

All I can say about parental pressure is that you have to balance your desire to be on your own with the gratitude you owe them for getting you started. It's a battle, there's no denying that. But sometimes it can work out beautifully. I will never forget looking over to my parents at the end of the 1985 U.S. Open. My parents, who had been watching so intensely that they looked as if they were at a funeral rather than a tennis match, were smiling and accepting the congratulations of the people around the box. I was so happy I can't describe it.

I'd also like to talk about playing tiebreakers and big points, which is when the pressure is really on.

Tiebreakers are generally won by the player with the best serve or the strongest momentum. An example of the latter was the tiebreaker at the end of the first set of the 1985 U.S. Open final. I came into the tiebreaker under control but confident. I stayed with my game plan, pressuring John from the baseline and coming to net when I had an opening. I steamrollered him, 7–1.

Take as much time as you can before a tiebreaker to come up with a strategy that takes momentum into account. If you have been coming from behind and have forced the breaker, look at the recent games and go with the strengths that got you to this point. If you can take your opponent out quickly, the tiebreaker can be a mental knockout. But this does not mean you have to play *fast*. Many young players confuse speed with pressure. If you go too fast, chances are you'll make mistakes, forget your strategy, and let your opponent back into the match.

If your opponent comes into the tiebreaker with the momentum, you've got a problem. But don't be so intimidated that you fail to come up with a strategy. Do anything you can to slow the pace of the match. Try to figure out what your opponent has been winning with. On what strengths has he been relying? What did he change in his game that turned the set around from yours to his? Use that time before the tiebreaker to take a deep breath and figure out how to counter his strengths.

Big points don't necessarily occur only in tiebreakers or at the end of the fifth set of a championship match. In fact, in most matches there will be several big points, often involving service breaks early on. In the 1985 U.S. Open final I lost a big point in the second game of the match, by double-faulting at ad-out. That put me down a break just five minutes into the match. But I recovered. And that's another thing to remember about big points: they may loom large at the time they're played, but once they're gone, forget about them.

I try not to alter my patterns too much on big

points. The toughest thing about big points is the pressure. I make sure I follow my routines before I play one of these points. If I'm serving, I'll use the sawdust, bounce the ball three or four times before I serve, just as I would before any point. If I'm receiving, I might walk back and towel off the racket handle, but other than that I do nothing to show the opponent that I'm overly concerned about this point.

Confidence on big points comes only with experience. Once you stay cool on a few big points and win, they become easier and easier to handle. Knowing that you've done it before, you know that you can do it again. And remember, the opponent is probably as nervous as you are. So take matters in hand and attack with the steady cool that keeps you hitting hot.

EXERCISE

I cannot emphasize too strongly the importance of physical conditioning. I'd like briefly to suggest a course of exercise that can head you in the right direction toward developing your own regimen.

Any tennis physique must have stamina and lower-body strength as its base. Exercises promoting these form the foundation for all your other exercises. It's no good developing quickness if you can't use that speed throughout an entire match.

Long-distance running should be the first step in building up proper tennis condition. Don't start off by running four or five miles, however. Start with a mile, or even a half mile. Build up from that in mile or half-mile increments, moving up only after you feel comfortable at the previous distance. Over Christmas, when I do my physical training, I usually do one or two hours a day of running, stretching, flexibility exercises, and sprints. While you needn't do that much, you should get to the point where you can comfortably run at least four miles at around eight minutes a mile.

You can build up leg strength through weight lifting, although you should be careful to pair this exercise with drills that emphasize flexibility. It's also important to work toward developing your stomach muscles, through sit-ups and leg-lifts. This can go hand in hand with weight lifting for the upper body, something I have come to recognize as very important.

But the central thing I have learned about tennis conditioning over the last couple of years is the importance of aerobics. I do aerobics for thirty minutes every day. When I'm home in Greenwich, I just go down to the local gym and work out with the women in their regular class. The dancing, stretching movements of aerobics are perfectly suited to tennis. Not only does aerobics help me maintain my stamina through the long tennis year, but it also offers me the flexibility I need for good footwork and for speed.

This isn't the place to describe a whole aerobics routine. You can find out about aerobics at any local gym, and I urge you to do so. Not only is this an exercise that will help your tennis game, but it may become an exercise you continue throughout your life.

NUTRITION

I have never had really bad eating habits. Oh, sure, when I came to the States for those Orange Bowl winters I'd stop in at fast-food joints from time to time, but on the whole, my diet was based on the old idea that athletes need lots of red meats and high-calorie proteins to fuel their high-energy life-styles. Then, at the time when Dr. Robert Haas and I were reshaping my diet, Tony Roche came along to reshape parts of my game. I lost fifteen pounds without sacrificing muscle, and in the process adopted an easy-to-follow diet that gives me the energy I need.

Before I go on to explain my diet and to suggest where you can go to learn more, I want to take a moment to emphasize the importance of good nutrition. The pursuit of tennis excellence shouldn't throw your life for a loop, of course. And diet seems like one of those things better left alone, one of those things that mostly concerns people who worry about fads. On top of all that, you may be in quite good shape, anyway. However, eating right is very important. If you lack the strength, stamina, and speed that a good diet gives you, your game will suffer accordingly.

If you're a younger player, you're still in a position to change your dietary habits without too much difficulty, and in so doing establish good patterns for the rest of your life. Take a look at Doctor Haas's diet. Then take a look at your own diet and make your own decision about changing. I think anyone who cares about tennis and about health will want to look *very* carefully at the Eat to Win Diet.

Essentially, the Eat to Win High-Energy Diet emphasizes complex carbohydrates. These are foods that are low in fat and proteins. Contrary to the old myths about red meat and high bulk, too many fats and proteins actually waste energy, making you feel sluggish. Complex carbohydrates, on the other hand, provide energy fast.

In general, the High-Energy Diet recommends the following combination of food types: 60–80 percent of daily calories from complex carbohydrates, 5–10 percent from simple carbohydrates, 10–15 percent from proteins, and 5–20 percent from fats. How much you should eat depends on many things, such as your age, your height and weight, and how much energy you expend during a normal day.

This isn't the place to go into the details of the plan. Essentially, however, in my effort to reach nutritional balance I take into consideration the following rules: I limit my consumption of high-fat meats, oils, butter, margarine, egg yolks, high-sodium foods, salt, and sugar. I eat more fiber foods, such as whole grains, cereals, and vegetables, and lean cuts of meat, poultry, and seafood.

One point about courtside nutrition. Those so-called thirst quenchers depend mostly on water for the so-called thirst-quenching miracles they perform. When you're thirsty, give your body what it really needs and wants: water.

If you are interested in a high-energy diet that has helped me (and several other prominent sports stars), take a look at Dr. Robert Haas's book, *Eat to Win: The Sports Nutrition Bible.* I hope you'll make proper nutrition a priority on your road to hitting hot.

EQUIPMENT

There's so much good equipment around now that there's really no reason, other than the obvious one of cost, for you to use equipment that will hurt your game. In this chapter I'd like to outline briefly some of the key points to remember when buying tennis equipment.

Buy clothing that's comfortable, neat, and durable. There's really no reason to try to show off on the tennis court when it comes to style. Likewise, there's no reason to look like a slob. In fact, an opponent looking at your sloppy clothing will probably take it as a reflection of your game, and perhaps gain some confidence from that. You should have tenniswear that is cool, that won't wear you down. For the same reason, I'd suggest bringing two shirts to any match you play. Sweatbands and headbands can also help you remain cool.

Your tennis shoes should be light and durable, and should fit well. A good pair of tennis shoes is usually worth the money. If your shoes are too heavy, you'll drag around the court, especially as you get toward the end of a longer match. I've worked with Adidas, my equipment company, to develop a shoe that's light and comfortable, and that has good traction on all kinds of surfaces.

Be sure that your racket feels right and that it is properly balanced. Most good pro shops will have demo rackets that you can try out before you have to buy. If your pro shop can't lend out rackets, borrow from friends. You should never buy a racket without first trying it out. Try out rackets of different sizes, too. The midsize rackets seem to be becoming the most popular. Oversize rackets are effective learning tools for beginners, but I tend to favor the midsize for tournament-level players. Look at the graphite rackets. The price is often prohibitive, but graphite offers a great blend of touch and power and can sometimes be found at a moderate price.

At any rate, don't be hasty in your purchase of a tennis racket. Try it out, on different surfaces, on all the strokes, with different types of opponents. With all the good equipment out there, you'll surely be able to find something that suits your game.

CODE OF CONDUCT: TENNIS ETIQUETTE

In the mid-seventies something happened to tennis etiquette. I don't pretend to know why it happened or who was responsible for the change. But all of a sudden tennis players seemed to be behaving poorly and getting away with it. Sure, this was partly the result of the tennis boom and the increased attention focused on tennis stars. But tennis was supposed to be one sport that still believed in proper conduct, and the fans were outraged.

I could see the change as I became a tournament player. When I was growing up in Czechoslovakia, anyone who dared to throw his racket would be summarily kicked out of the club, let alone off the court. There was little tolerance of poor behavior, and perhaps as a result there was little poor behavior.

I've had my problems with umpires and linesmen, and it's one of the areas of my game that I have tried to improve. One of the reasons for this is that I am distressed by the fact that a tendency toward outrageous court manners has extended deep into the junior ranks. I am proud of my on-court behavior, and I hope it is a model for younger players. With few well-mannered pros to look up to, there's really no reason for the juniors to contain themselves.

But I think the outrage on the part of the tennis public is helping to turn the tide toward better court etiquette. I urge you to control your temper on the court. Not only will this reflect well on you, it will improve your game. Any time you let your temper get the best of you, you lose the ability to concentrate on your game.

There are times when you can argue a call. If you're sure a call is incorrect, there's no reason not to ask about it politely, whether you're questioning your opponent or an umpire. On the whole, however, remember that umpires and linesmen are fallible but impartial people who will probably make mistakes the other way as well. In the long run, you will probably get as many calls in your favor as against you.

If you're in a tournament without linesmen, I'd recommend the following pattern if you're up against an opponent you think might be cheating. The first time he makes a questionable call, just ask him if he's sure. The second time, question him again and warn him that you are thinking of asking for a line judge. The third time, go ahead and ask one of the tournament supervisors or directors for a line judge.

Don't try to disrupt your opponent's game with meaningless tirades or silly displays of temper. There are other, less offensive, more effective ways of psyching out your opponent. People just don't respect that kind of behavior.

Finally, court etiquette is a matter of conscience. It's fine to be questioning, as long as you are polite. Proper court etiquette can only help your game.

SUMMARY

In the fourteen days of this clinic we have covered all the different aspects of "hitting hot," from the specifics of ground strokes to ideas about tournament preparation. I hope I've introduced you to a new, dominating playing style. And I hope I've introduced myself to you along the way.

While it would be impossible for me to summarize everything we've done here, I would like to reemphasize the most important points of this clinic.

First of all, I can't say enough about the importance of good physical condition. Tennis is dominated now by an all-court pressure game, an unrelenting but controlled brand of tennis that is impossible to play successfully if you're out of shape. In reworking my game, Tony Roche and I have placed prime importance on my physical condition. Part of this has involved the high-carbohydrate diet created by Dr. Robert Haas. But in addition, Tony and I felt that I needed to develop my physique. I've done lots of aerobics and speed work, and I have worked to get myself into shape.

As a result, the game is more fun for me. Now that I'm in peak physical shape I can work harder and enjoy the game more because I don't get tired. Tennis is a game now, and not work. And I think that's the key to my success. Now I'm out there playing and having fun instead of looking at the clock and saying "It feels like an hour and a half out here and it's only been ten minutes." The way it's been for me recently, it's been an hour and a half before I think of taking myself off the court so I don't overplay myself.

Hand in hand with physical conditioning goes practice. From childhood on, I've made every effort I could to get practice time. Use that time to good purpose by planning it carefully. In this clinic I've suggested just a few of the thousands of station drills you can use with one or more partners. But more than just picking out certain specific drills, you should use practice to effect specific changes in your game.

Many players are afraid to change their game. I suppose I too was afraid to experiment for a while. I was relying on a big forehand and a tough flat serve, and these were taking me pretty far. But deep inside I knew that I wanted more from myself as a tennis player, and that improvement would come only with change. And so Tony and I went to work, changing my strategy, working on my net game. And the result came together at the U.S. Open, where I felt comfortable both at the net and at the baseline.

I still practice at least three hours a day on nonmatch days. And while much of my practice is intended to reinforce my best strokes, much of it is devoted to trying out new things, to working on my weaknesses. You can never practice too much. But undirected, mindless practice is of no help whatsoever. So you need to develop an ability to analyze your own game. I believe that the best way to analyze your own game is to look at it as if you were a coach looking at someone else's play. This analysis should be both specific and long-term. When you're down in a match, you need to be able to step away from yourself and look carefully at what you are doing wrong. People have told me that they can tell when I'm doing this. I'm drawn tight and concentrating so hard I don't notice anything going on around me. But when I do that during the changeovers, I can come back onto the court with a new perspective on my game and a new, more intense desire to win.

You need to look at your game over the long run in the same way. This sort of dispassionate examination of your game may be painful at times. You may see that you're relying on only one or two weapons, or that you've been trying to get away with lazy footwork. But it's better to face up to the need to change than to continue with the same strokes just because you didn't take the time to analyze your game carefully.

My final point is—have fun. Enjoy this amazing game. Maybe that sounds corny to some of you, but I think it's terribly important. If you're not having fun, you can't be a good judge of your game. You're probably forcing yourself through some awful practices, and you probably hate those training runs that seem pointless and always too long. Having fun does not mean your practices are going to be frivolous. It doesn't mean you'll be the dupe of every tough guy who walks around the tournament grounds with an implacable frown. What it does mean is that you'll have tennis in perspective, and that with that added perspective you'll be able to improve your game.

Look, tennis is finally just a game. It's a beautiful, graceful, athletic, and demanding one, to be sure, but in the big scheme of things it's just a game. And for that very reason, there's no point in playing it without trying your hardest to play it as well as you can. Tennis just gets better and better the more you play and the more you improve. And in a way, that's what *Hitting Hot* is all about: getting the most out of this amazing game.

Ryan and I take a break to discuss our net play. My final point is Have fun!

IVAN LENDL

Birthdate:	March 7, 1960	Height:	6'2"
Birthplace:	Ostrava, Czechoslovakia	Weight:	175 lbs.
Residence:	Greenwich, Connecticut	Plays:	Right-handed
	Gleneagles Country Club, Delray Beach, Florida		

CAREER HIGHLIGHTS

Champion, U.S. Open, Flushing Meadow, N.Y., 1985; finalist, 1982, 1983, 1984

Champion, French Open, Paris, France, 1984, 1986; finalist, 1981, 1985

Finalist, Australian Open, Melbourne, Australia, 1983

Semifinalist, All England Championships, Wimbledon, England, 1983, 1984

Champion at nine tournaments in 1985 including the WCT Tournament of Champions at Forest Hills, N.Y., U.S. Clay Court Championships, Monte Carlo Open, Paine Webber Classic, WCT Finals, and U.S. Open

Champion, WCT Finals, Dallas, Texas, 1982, 1985; finalist, 1983

Champion, Grand Prix Masters, New York, 1982, 1983, 1986; finalist, 1981, 1984, 1985

Champion, Lipton International Players Championships, 1985

Set all-time prize record by earning $2,028,850 in 1982

Established Volvo Grand Prix record by winning five tournaments in as many weeks; also won the Volvo Grand Prix bonus pool, 1981, 1985

Compiled 45-match winning streak—second longest in men's open tennis history—while winning eight straight singles titles, September 1981–February 1982

Member, Czechoslovakian Davis Cup teams, 1980–1985, including the team that won the Cup in 1980

World's top junior player in 1978, winning Wimbledon, French, Italian, and Orange Bowl junior championships

ABOUT THE AUTHORS

IVAN LENDL was born in Ostrava, Czechoslovakia, in 1960. Both his parents were ranked tennis players, and he began playing the game as a small child. He joined the professional tennis circuit in 1978, winning many junior tournaments that year. In 1980 he led the Czechoslovakian team to victory in the Davis Cup. Ivan then went on to win the Masters Tournament in 1982 and 1983, and his first Grand Slam tournament, the French Open, in 1984. He won nine tournaments in 1985, including the U.S. Open, and established himself firmly as the world's number-one player. Ivan now lives in Greenwich, Connecticut.

GEORGE MENDOZA has written and produced more than one hundred books during his active and varied career in publishing. He has collaborated with Norman Rockwell, Marcel Marceau, Andrés Segovia, Michel Legrand, Carol Burnett, Zero Mostel, and Pope John Paul II. Mendoza has also been honored by Time *magazine, the* New York Times *and the Museum of Modern Art for his work in children's literature. In a very unusual tribute to a living writer, Boston University has established a George Mendoza library, which contains all of his works and papers, as part of its Twentieth-Century Archives. George is a keen tennis player, but he says he can no longer keep up with his son, Ryan, who was Ivan Lendl's pupil during the making of this book.*